QUANTUM NOTES

Whole-Brain Approaches to Note-Taking

by

Bobbi DePorter
with Mike Hernacki

Learning Forum Publications
Oceanside, California USA

LEARNING FORUM PUBLICATIONS
1938 Avenida del Oro
Oceanside, CA 92056 USA
(760) 722-0072
(760) 305-7766 fax
email: info@QLN.com
www.QLN.com

Cover design by Kelley Thomas
Illustrations by Ellen Duris

ISBN: 0-945525-21-4

*Dedicated to all the very special Quantum Learning Network
staff who over the years have contributed so much.*

Whole-Brain Approaches to Note-Taking

 What is the main purpose of note-taking—and what other purposes can it serve?

 What is Mind Mapping and how does it work?

 What are Mindscapes?

 What is Notes:TM and how is it better than traditional note-taking?

Contents

1

Who Takes Notes?

Effective note-taking is one of the most important skills anyone ever learns. For students, it often means the difference between scoring high or low at test time. For business people, it can mean keeping track of important tasks and projects instead of getting lost in a sea of scattered slips of paper.

"Mental notes" don't work because the brain focuses on whatever is vying for its attention at a particular moment. And even when we do remember a "mental note," it often comes back to us in the same fuzzy, haphazard way we stored it in our brains originally. So if you want to remember something—if you *have* to remember it—write it down.

You probably already do take notes—those hurried, incomprehensible scribbles which end up being of little or no use to you or anyone else. But what if you knew how to take notes that really meant something? Imagine taking notes that capture entire concepts, organize information, make connections between ideas, are easy to remember, and fun to take: that's the kind of note-taking this book focuses on. Forget the traditional outline format you learned in school. You're about to master Mind Mapping®, Mindscaping, and Notes:TM—easy, effective note-taking systems that can record volumes of information on a single page.

You take some kind of notes every day. It could be in the form of recording what was discussed at a meeting, jotting down the key ideas from a school lecture, or just making out your to-do list. The main purpose of note-taking is to help you understand and remember valuable information. A good note-taking method can help you keep track of the latest breakthroughs in your field, and can also help you stay on top of the myriad projects, activities, and meetings you're involved in every day.

The main purpose of note-taking is to help you remember and understand valuable information.

Easy and effective note-taking systems include:

Mind Mapping®

∷

Mindscaping

∷

Notes: TM

We've all taken notes at seminars, classes or meetings to record events and ideas. But note-taking has other applications. Besides recording information, you can also use note-taking to generate fresh ideas and organize your thoughts. You can use notes as a starting point for writing papers, articles, reports, speeches, even your own books. They may also spark your creativity and ease mental blocks. The applications are endless, so let's get started.

2

Mind Mapping®

Y ou may already have been exposed to the note-taking method called Mind Mapping®, that is catching on fast around the world. It was developed by Tony Buzan in the early '70's while lecturing on psychology and memory at various universities. In *The Mind Map Book* (Dutton, New York, 1994), he says:

> "I began to notice the enormous discrepancy between the theory I was teaching and what I was actually doing. My lecture notes were traditional linear notes, providing the traditional amount of non-communication. I was using such notes as the basis of lectures on memory in which I was pointing out that two of the main factors in recall were association and emphasis. Yet these elements were singularly lacking in my own notes!"

This realization spurred him to develop a better note-taking system based on brain research—Mind Mapping. This method works well because it imitates the way your brain works. Like many of the methods used throughout this book, Mind Mapping engages both the left and right hemispheres of the brain. Pictures, symbols, colors, and random ordering, primarily right hemisphere activities, are incorporated into this system, as is the left-hemisphere processing of words, logic and sequences.

Research shows there are five key elements to making facts memorable. We learn best when information:
1. Is emphasized,
2. Is associated with prior learning,
3. Engages our five senses,

I started this book by creating a Mind Map® so I could see how all of the information fit together.

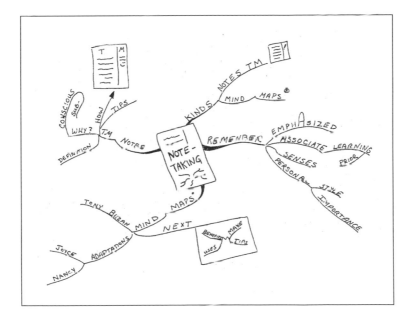

Here's my Mind Map for this book.

4. Has personal importance, or

5. Comes at the beginning or end of the learning period.

Mind Mapping makes use of all these elements, resulting in some powerful, highly memorable note-taking! (You can read more about the power of your memory in *Quantum Memory: Working Magic with Your Memory.*)

Take a moment now and look at the page to the right. Close your eyes and picture an apple on that page. (Do this now.)

Where did you picture the apple on the page? In the upper right corner? Lower left? In the center? Was your picture black-and-white or color?

Most people will picture things in the center of the page and in color. That's how the brain stores information. Naturally, the best notes work *with* your brain rather than against it.

Now look at the Mind Map on the previous page. (It's a Mind Map of notes for this book.) Study it for a minute.

Now, test yourself. Look away or cover it up and ask yourself the following questions:

- What are the titles of the four main branches?
- Where does the arrow point?
- What are tips to better help us remember?

You may amaze yourself by remembering all or most of these things—even if you've always considered yourself poor at noticing details. It's easy to remember details from a Mind Map because it's written in a form that your brain naturally follows.

Mind Mapping® is a whole-brain approach using visual images and other graphic devices to form impressions.

Close your eyes and imagine an apple on this page.

Getting Started

First, take all your old ideas about note-taking, such as linear format, Roman numerals, single-coloring, and so on—and throw them away. You won't need any of that. Now, take a look at the Mind Map model on the right-hand page. Notice how it starts with a central idea and branches out to include subtopics and details. The lines of the main topics are thicker to emphasize their importance. Keep in mind that these main branches are usually different colors, although this book is printed in black and white. Also notice the use of symbols and pictures to communicate thoughts. When you get the hang of Mind Mapping, you'll probably develop your own pictorial shorthand, conveying reams of information in minimal space.

One of the best things about Mind Maps is that you can keep adding thoughts as they come to mind. Linear notes, such as lists, limit our thinking. They make it difficult for us to make associations, the very process we use to generate new ideas. With Mind Maps, when we have more ideas we just add more branches, so our original Mind Map can spawn a dozen other Mind Maps. We can also make associations between two different topics, as you can see in our model Mind Map.

Practice making a few Mind Maps of your own. You can Mind Map any topic: plans for your next vacation, the last book you read, school lectures, ideas for a report or anything else that comes to mind. The key right now is practice.

Follow These Simple Steps

To begin, you'll need colored pens or pencils and a piece of paper. Turning your paper in a horizontal or "landscape" position makes it easier to create your Mind Map; it gives

To Mind Map®, focus on a central idea and "branch" outward.

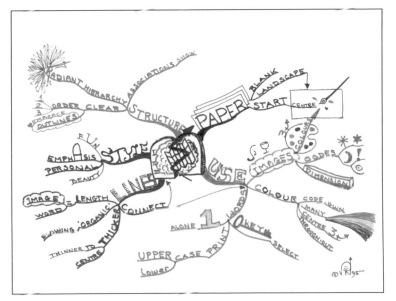

– by Vanda North

you more room to draw horizontal branches, which makes them easier to read.

1. *Put Your Main Topic in the Center of the Page*
     It can be a written word, a drawing, or both. Using a drawing may make the Mind Map more powerful and increase your ability to remember it, especially if you're the type who thinks better in pictures than in words (you know who you are).

2. *Draw a Thick Branch Extending Out from the Main Idea for Each of Your Subtopics or Key Points*
     Make each branch a different color, or rotate colors to keep it varied. Avoid making two side-by-side branches the same color; different colors help make it easier to distinguish between subtopics. Write the key word or image on top of each branch. Try to stick to one word as it provides more freedom of thought.

3. *Attach New Branches to Your Subtopics as You Come Up with Thoughts on These Areas*
     Using pictures and symbols makes your Mind Map more memorable. Place them on the line as well.

   You may discover that one of your smaller points is really a main topic that you'd like to explore further by making it a separate Mind Map. That is the nature of Mind Maps. They allow for leaps in thought and associations, and they encourage creativity.

   Mind Maps are a great way to overcome mental blocks; those frustrating moments when you seem to run out of ideas. Because the brain searches for completion and likes to see the whole picture, you can defeat mental

Mind Map® Laws

- Start in the center with an image of the topic, using at least three colors.

- Use images, symbols, and codes throughout.

- Select keys words.

- Print one word only on each main or extending branch.

- Make the lines the same length as the word or image.

- Connect main lines to the central image, making them thicker at the start and becoming thinner as they radiate out.

- Use a different color for each main branch (or rotate colors) and keep the same color for extending branches.

blocks simply by adding empty branches to your Mind Map. Your brain will naturally search for associations to fill in the blanks.

This trick is especially helpful when you're faced with a writing assignment and don't know where to begin. Make a Mind Map of your letter or article, putting your topic in the center. Ask yourself what the main points are, and make these your branches. Draw smaller branches from these main points, and let your mind fill in the blanks. You'll quickly have all your thoughts down on paper and will be able to then put them in order. This method is used successfully by many professional writers to get past "writer's block" and is useful for anyone.

Putting Mind Maps to Work

Once you are comfortable using Mind Maps, you'll want to start using them whenever you can. I suggest you start using Mind Maps at brainstorming sessions at school or work. It's a great way to record everyone's thoughts, get the creative juices flowing, and generate lots of fresh ideas.

At my company, we have a meeting every fall to review our summer programs. Prior to the meeting, we ask staff members to record their thoughts on individual Mind Maps. Then, we combine all the Mind Maps into one. This way, everyone's input is posted where we can all review it, and the meeting runs more efficiently.

For those of you in the business world, consultant Joyce Wycoff has written an entire book on the business applications of Mind Maps. In *Mind Mapping, Your Personal Guide to Exploring Creativity and Problem-Solving,* (Berkley Books, New York, 1991), she describes how five minutes of Mind Mapping can move you toward better project management, a method used by many businesses

Six Tips for Mind Mapping®

1   **Print neatly.** Emphasize words through under-lining, highlighting, and thick lines.

2   **Show associations by drawing an arrow between branches.**

3   **Personalize your Mind Map by relating information to your own experiences.** I find there's something personal about the process of making Mind Maps. Creating my own Mind Map forces me to come up with my own symbols and connections, cementing the information in my memory.

4   **Develop your own shorthand of symbols, pictures, and abbreviations.**

5   **Unleash your natural artistic ability.** Add lots of pictures to your Mind Map. Your drawings will improve with practice.

6   **When you've completed your Mind Map, you may want to put the information in either chronological order or in order of importance.** To do this, simply number each branch. On my own Mind Maps, I always start my first branch in the upper right, the one o'clock position, and continue clockwise. This way, my information is already in order, and when I review my Mind Maps I always know where to start.

these days. She notes, "The increased focus on projects (versus repetitive processes) is one of the biggest changes in work life today. Everyone has become a project manager." If you feel reluctant to start a project, drawing a Mind Map can help get you going.

Starting out with a Mind Map gives you direction, and it can make overwhelming projects more manageable. A Mind Map forces you to break a project down into smaller chunks, or sub-projects, thereby making it easier to master. You can then calculate your action steps and delegate the sub-projects.

Making a project management Mind Map is really quite simple. Use the usual Mind Map format, putting your main topic in the center with subtopics branching out. Then, in the upper left corner, write WWWWWH$. This stands for Who, What, When, Where, Why, How and Money. Wycoff suggests referring to this list while making your Mind Map. Ask yourself: Who needs to be involved in the project, What resources are needed, When does it need to be completed, What costs are involved, and other related questions.

Asking these questions will help you think through the project thoroughly. It will also spur you to overcome any mental blocks. Once you've completed your Mind Map, it's easy to move forward with your project.

You can also use Mind Maps to record notes, create agendas and schedules, or organize your thoughts. The applications are endless. Introduce your colleagues and friends to this method and start putting it to work for yourself, too. Before long, it may become the natural note-taking method for everyone you know.

Uses of
Mind Maps®

Learning

Overviewing

Concentrating

Memorizing

Organizing

Presenting

Communicating

Planning

Project Management

Meetings

Training

Thinking

Reviewing

Benefits of Mind Mapping

It's Flexible. If a speaker suddenly remembers to make a point about a previous thought, you can easily add it to the appropriate place on your Mind Map without creating confusion.

It Focuses Attention. You're not concerned with catching every word that is said. Instead, you can concentrate on ideas.

It Increases Understanding. When you're reading a text or technical report, Mind Mapping increases your understanding and provides great review notes for later.

It's Fun. Your imagination and creativity are limitless, and that makes taking and reviewing notes more fun.

Benefits of
Mind Mapping®

It's flexible.

::

It focuses attention.

::

It increases understanding.

::

It's fun.

3

Mindscapes

Mindscapes are an outgrowth of Mind Mapping. Developed by Nancy Margulies, corporate consultant and author, this method goes beyond the rules of Mind Mapping, allowing further individuality. Once you've mastered Mind Mapping, you may want to experiment with this unique method.

Steps

1. The first rule of Mindscapes is, it's okay to break the rules. Breaking rules encourages creativity.

2. Start anywhere on the page. A Mindscape doesn't necessarily need a central image; it's a more free-flowing form of visual mapping, so do whatever works.

3. Mindscape images may incorporate words, phrases, quotations, even photos or pictures from magazines.

4. Vary your Mindscapes as much as possible. Experiment with different forms. Develop your own style.

Nancy is a visual mapper with clout. As a consultant, she has Mindscaped meetings for hundreds of companies, including Xerox, Boeing, and Hewlett-Packard. She also teaches Mindscaping and mapping at seminars and conferences.

I once scheduled Nancy to Mindscape at the annual Accelerative Learning and Teaching conference. As president of the International Alliance for Learning, I knew Nancy would add much to the conference. Unfortunately, someone else also wanted her talents. Two weeks before

Mindscaping is a note-taking method drawing on your individuality.

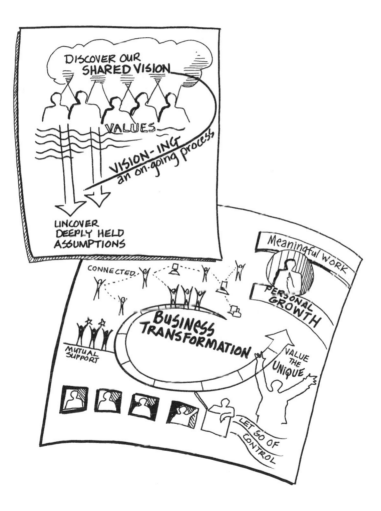

Nancy Margulies developed this unique method of recording information in a highly visual format.

the conference, I received a call from Nancy. Apologetically, she told me she wouldn't be able to make it. She'd received an invitation to map a meeting for someone she couldn't turn down: President Clinton.

Nancy Mindscaped a retreat meeting that included the President, Vice-President, and members of the Cabinet. Nancy says she was called in because, "They wanted to be able to convey the essence of the discussion to their own staffs, and experience sharing information in both an auditory and visual way. They understood that it is necessary to reach people on many levels."

I was sorry she missed my conference, but really couldn't blame her. For most of us, an invitation to present our work to the President is a once-in-a-lifetime experience.

4

Notes: TM

N otes:TM is a variation of Cornell Notes, and was developed by a Quantum Learning facilitator, Mark Reardon. The TM stands for Taking and Making. Note-*Taking* is writing down the information you want to remember. Note-*Making* is writing down your own thoughts and impressions about that information. Putting the two together helps you focus on the information at hand and makes it more meaningful for you. One of the keys to remembering something is giving it personal importance.

Here's a common situation where Notes:TM could come to the rescue. Picture a typical meeting or class. It's three o'clock in the afternoon, and you're feeling a little drowsy. The speakers drone on and on. What they have to say is important, but your mind keeps drifting. You think about what you ate for lunch, what you'll do afterwards, even your own projects. Suddenly, you notice the room is quiet. The speaker turns to you and says "What's your opinion on this?" Desperately, you search your notes for a clue of what was said, but all you find is a blank page.

Why do our minds drift despite our best efforts to pay attention? Because the average person's normal speaking rate doesn't keep up with our brain's ability to process information. The normal speaking rate is approximately 200 to 300 words per minute. Our brains are able to process auditory information at 600 to 800 words per minute. Because of the lag-time created and our minds' ability to make associations, we're able to think about all sorts of things while listening to someone speak. Notes:TM can help you turn your mind's wanderings to your advantage.

By writing down both the speaker's information and your own thoughts and impressions about what's being said, you're focusing both your conscious and subconscious

Notes: TM helps you focus on information and makes it more meaningful.

Notes: TM

T is for Taking
Writing down the information you want to remember

M is for Making
Writing down your own thoughts and impressions

mind. When you're focusing on the speaker's words and writing down factual data, you're using your conscious mind. The subconscious is where you make associations, form impressions, reactions, or new applications to the information. Writing down your subconscious thoughts helps you keep focused on the task at hand.

Recent studies have shown the effectiveness of this technique. Win Wenger, a learning and creativity consultant, conducted experiments on a note-taking method he calls Freenoting™. Students were told to write rapidly in the context of the topic, even if they were sure they knew nothing about it! As they wrote, they were to consciously ignore the lecture being presented. The study showed that these students still wrote down clear notes on the lecture topic. In fact, they usually put down more and better information than the lecturer had presented! According to Wenger, "The exercise locks in and makes richly memorable the essential contents of the lecture. By consciously ignoring the lecturer's words, the Freenoter was sending the contents of what the lecturer was saying directly to the subconscious." Ignoring the lecture frees the mind, allowing for associations and connections that might be missed if the student were consciously paying attention. Associations made in the subconscious mind made the lecture much more memorable than if the students had simply listened on a conscious level.

Notes:TM—How To Do It

On a sheet of paper, draw a vertical line dividing the sheet so that three-quarters of the page is to the left of the line. Now, use the larger left side for Note-Taking—copying down what's being said. The right-hand side is where you

Notes: TM applies both the conscious and subconscious minds to the material at hand.

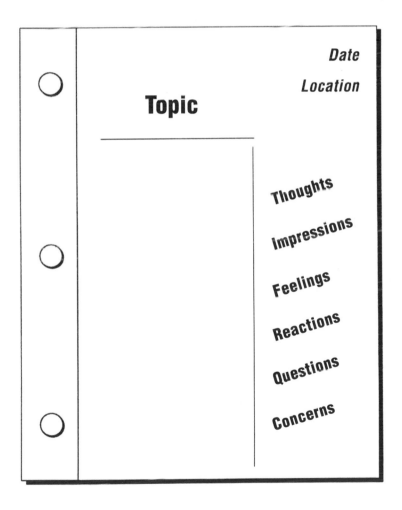

Date

Location

Topic

Thoughts

Impressions

Feelings

Reactions

Questions

Concerns

jot down your own impressions about the information—Note-Making.

Use two different colored pens and switch colors whenever the speaker changes topics. This will make it easier to remember your notes and to review them later on. When using the Notes:TM technique, take a minute or two after the presentation or lecture to go back over your notes and add your own personal graphics—symbols and pictures that are meaningful to you. It's best to make up your own symbols, but here are some ideas to help you get started:

!=important point
arrow=connection to something else on the page
smiley face=positive
sad face=negative
3X=repeated 3 times (must be important!)

The symbols can mean whatever you want them to mean. However, stay with the same symbols and meanings once you have a system.

When you review your notes, the symbols trigger your mind to remember what the speaker was saying as well as relive what you were thinking at the time, consciously and subconsciously. Often, the most valuable thing we get from a meeting, speech, or lecture is not the material itself but the ideas it sparks in our minds.

I've found that the Notes:TM technique works best for taking notes during a speech, meeting, or class. It can also work well for taking notes on reading material. The principle and the process are much the same. The major difference is that when you're reading, you're going at your

Symbols trigger ideas, recall the speaker's comments, and help to bring back thoughts about the presentation.

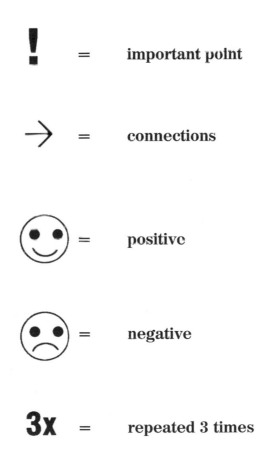

!	=	important point
→	=	connections
☺	=	positive
☹	=	negative
3x	=	repeated 3 times

own pace and you don't have to worry that your note-*making* is causing you to miss any of the material you're getting in your note-*taking*.

Notes:TM Tips

1. *Record Your Feelings/Emotions about Information* (boring, sad, exciting, etc.). Creating an emotional relationship to the information makes it easier to recall.

2. *Personalize Your Notes with Symbols and Pictures* Develop your own system of symbols.

3. *Review the Highlighted Portions of Your Notes Periodically to Cement Them in Your Memory*

4. *Follow Up on Any Ideas Recorded on Either Side of Your Page* Your subconscious ramblings just may be the beginning of something great!

Benefits of Notes:TM

It's Easier To Remember a subject when you read what you were thinking about at the time.

It Focuses Your Emotions and helps you tap into your emotional memory.

It's Constructive Daydreaming. It occupies your mind and makes you aware of your thoughts and of where they are drifting, so you can bring them back and stay more in control. (This helps you when you feel the speaker isn't talking fast enough or saying enough to keep your interest.)

Under Note-Making,
record your thoughts
and feelings. Add images.

Note: Taking	Note: Making
🔑 KEY POINTS: text, text, text, text, text, text, text, text, text, text, text, text, text, text, text,	Impressions . . . etc, etc, etc, etc, etc, etc, etc, etc
INFORMATION: text, text, text ✻ text, text, text, text, text, text, text, text, text, text, text, text, text, text, text, text, text, text,	Thoughts . . . etc, etc, etc, etc, etc, etc, etc. ♥
FACT: text, text, text, text, text, text, text, text, text, text, text, text, text, text, $ text, text, text, text, text, text, text, text, text, text, text.	Will this really work? etc, etc, etc, etc, etc, etc, etc, etc
FACT: text, text, text, text, text, text, text, text, text, ! text, text, text, text, text, text, text, text, text, text, text.	

It Records Your Judgments, making you more aware of them so you can be more open to seeing another side. It's especially helpful to write down when you disagree with the speaker or don't believe what the speaker is saying. You can say to yourself, "I may disagree, but I can listen and keep an open mind while he is speaking."

Benefits of Notes: TM

It's easier to remember
a subject.

⋮

It focuses your emotions.

⋮

It's constructive daydreaming.

⋮

It records your judgments.

5

Practice & More Tips

Practice, Practice, Practice

Mind Mapping, Mindscaping, and Notes:TM may feel awkward to you at first. You may worry that you're missing valuable information by just drawing a picture or jotting down your feelings. When I first started Mind Mapping, I wasn't sure it was going to work. But I committed to trying it for one week, and I practiced every chance I got. I Mind Mapped books, articles, speeches, anything I could. During that process, the method became easy and natural.

More Note-Taking Tips

Regardless of what method you use, here are some tips that can help you take more effective notes:

Listen Actively

Ask yourself, "What does the speaker expect me to learn? Why? What is he saying? How does it relate to the subject? Is it important? Is it something I need to be sure to remember?" Asking these questions makes it easier to select and separate what is important from what is unimportant. If you use the Notes:TM approach, this provides you with a steady supply of things to jot down on the right side of the line.

Always summarize important and meaningful information and ideas that you need to retain, remember, and use. Notes should focus on material that's important or will be needed later.

Observe Actively

Pay attention to clues you can pick up from the speaker and your reading material. Clues in the reading material can take the form of headings, bold type, italics, pictures,

Practice Note-Taking Approaches

Mind Mapping®

Imitates the way your brain works.

Mindscaping

A free-flowing form that draws on your individuality.

Notes: TM

Recording information plus *your thoughts, feeling and impressions.*

graphs, and diagrams. Some books have chapter outlines that contain important topics. Look at section and chapter summaries. Note the author's or speaker's conclusions. Look for physical clues from the speaker too. Every speaker has a unique style; you can pick up on important points by becoming familiar with that style. Activate your antennae to the speaker's facial expressions, gestures, body movements, and raised or lowered voice. Notice when she repeats an idea or word, and be attentive to what she writes on the board. Always sit as close to the front of the room as possible—it's easier to pick up on important clues that way.

Participate

If you don't understand something or have a question about it, ask. Join in discussions. Some people hold back, worrying about what others might think. Surveys show that people in an audience usually think highly of participators, often envying them for their courage even when they resent them for interrupting. Besides, what's the worst other people can think—that you're selfish in wanting to gain new knowledge?

Preview

If you know what a speaker or lecturer is going to discuss, preview the material and find as much information on it as possible beforehand. Having some knowledge ahead of time will help you identify important points during a speech or lecture.

You'll also know which concepts are unclear to you, so you can be prepared to ask questions. As you hear bits of information, you'll find it easier to see how they fit together in

More Tips on Note-Taking

❖ Listen actively

❖ Observe actively

❖ Participate

❖ Preview

❖ Make the auditory visual

❖ Make reviewing easy

❖ Commit to giving it a chance

the big picture. Previewing is one of the most effective ways to insure success and understanding.

I know you're thinking, "Who has time to preview?" The answer to that is, previewing actually takes very little time. Often just a few moments scanning an agenda or looking over notes from a previous meeting is all you'll need to do. All your mind needs is a little stimulation.

Make the Auditory Visual

Your notes should be personal and meaningful to you, just like snapshots. Have you ever noticed how a snapshot from a vacation or important event brings a flood of memories—things you thought you'd forgotten?

When you're taking in information, snap pictures of it by adding visual associations like symbols, drawings, and arrows as they occur to you. This way, your notes, even if reviewed months later, will remind you instantly of the material you knew was important at the time—and need to recall now.

Make Reviewing Easy

When taking/making notes, write on only one side of the paper. Use single sheets, not paper in a bound notebook. Then you can lay the sheets out in front of you or hang them up on the wall later, when you need to review.

Copy key notes on three-by-five cards that you can carry around with you. When you're standing in line, riding a bus, or waiting for an appointment, you can take them out for a few minutes of extra study or thinking time.

Commit yourself to practicing Mind Mapping®, Mindscaping, and Notes:TM for one week.

These new note-taking methods will soon become easy and natural.

Commit to Giving It a Chance

I recommend you also commit yourself to a week of trying Mind Mapping, Mindscaping, or Notes:TM. Try a few practice exercises so you get the hang of using these approaches. For instance, take notes on a book you're reading, recording key points and your own impressions. Or, take notes while listening to a taped lecture, a radio show, or while watching the news. Experiment with various colors and symbols. Soon you'll be up to speed and ready for your important meeting or class. The more you practice these skills, the easier and more natural they'll become.

Celebrate Your Learning!

! *What is the main purpose of note-taking and what other purposes can it serve?*
Its main purpose is to help you understand and remember valuable information. But it can also help you generate fresh ideas, organize your thoughts, spark your creativity, and help you overcome mental blocks.

! *What is Mind Mapping and how does it work?*
It is a note-taking method that imitates the way the brain works in order to make your notes more memorable, useful, and valuable.

! *What are Mindscapes?*
These are a more free-flowing form of visual mapping, allowing for further individuality.

! *What is Notes:TM and how is it better than traditional note-taking?*
Notes:TM stands for Notes: Taking and Making. It's better because it distinguishes between noting the information you receive (note-taking) and your reactions to it (note-making).

Since 1981, Quantum Learning Network (QLN) has produced educational programs for students, educators and business. Its vision is to create a shift in how people learn, so that learning will be joyful, challenging, engaging and meaningful.

Programs and products of QLN —

QUANTUM LEARNING PROGRAMS

Quantum Learning is a comprehensive model of effective learning and teaching. Its programs include: **Quantum Learning for Teachers**, professional development programs for educators providing a proven, research-based approach to the design and delivery of curriculum and the teaching of learning and life skills; **Quantum Learning for Administrators**, programs for enhancing leadership skills, productive team building, keeping teachers resourceful, and establishing a positive, productive atmosphere; **Quantum Learning for Students,** programs that help students master powerful learning and life skills; and **Quantum Learning for Business,** working with companies and organizations to shift training and cultural environments to ones that are both nurturing and effective.

SUPERCAMP

The most innovative and unique program of its kind, SuperCamp incorporates proven, leading-edge learning methods that help students succeed through the mastery of academic, social and everyday life skills. Programs are held across the U.S. on college campuses, as well as inter-nationally, for four age levels: Youth Forum (9-10), Junior Forum (11-13), Senior Forum (14-18), and Quantum U (18-24).

SUCCESS PRODUCTS

QLN has brought together a collection of books, video/audio tapes and CDs believed to be the most effective for accelerating growth and learning. Visit www.QLN.com to view the complete line of products.

For information contact:

QLN𝑄 quantum learning network™

1938 Avenida del Oro, Oceanside, CA 92056
760.722.0072 • 800.285.3276 • Fax 760.305.7766
email: products@QLN.com • www.QLN.com

Bobbi DePorter's career path began at Hawthorne/Stone Real Estate and Investments in San Fr ancisco, where in a short time she went from agent to junior partner and became a millionaire. She went on to co-found the Burklyn Business School and was so intrigued with how people learn, she studied with Dr. Georgi Lozanov, founder of accelerated learning, and applied his methods at the school. She later co-founded Quantum Learning Network, a company now headquartered in Oceanside, California. Quantum Learning Network produces SuperCamp, learning-to-learn and self-esteem programs for youth; trains educators in Quantum Learning methods; and works with major companies to shift training environments and corporate culture. Programs are held across the United States and internationally. Bobbi's first book, *Quantum Learning: Unleashing the Genius in You,* continues to influence the expansion of Quantum Learning programs and draws interest from around the world. Bobbi has also served as president of the International Alliance for Learning, the leading networking association dedicated to accelerated learning. She resides in the San Diego area with her husband, Joe Chapon, who is also her partner at Quantum Learning Network.

Mike Hernacki, a former teacher, attorney, and stockbroker, has been a freelance writer and marketing consultant since 1979. He is the author of four books: *The Ultimate Secret to Getting Absolutely Everything You want, The Secret to Conquering Fear, The Forgotten Secret to Phenomenal Success,* and *The Secret to Permanent Prosperity.* His books have been translated into six languages and are sold all over the world. He now divides his time between writing and personal success coaching.